BRAAI
★ THE ★
BELOVED
COUNTRY

★ JEAN NEL ★

JACANA

THANKS

The braai in my being is a strong fire and I am determined to never let it be extinguished. Mauritzio Grossi, thank you for believing in me, for your faith, courage and support. No event or project is numero uno without you. And thank you to Keith Barclay who made this wonderful walk possible.

Kelly Ramsay, thank you that you allow me to use The Good Food Studio as my playground.

Russel Wasserfall, it's a dream come true working with you. The photos are superb.

Camilla Comins, your attention to detail with the food styling is out of this world.

Alex Brodbeck, thank you for your generosity. Marriane wine farm is captured in my heart.

The Jacana ladies, wow, what a team!

To my staff... I am blessed to have you with me.

To the millions of South Africans that light their fires... Braai, the Beloved Country!

CONTENTS

Wherever specified, salt means flaked sea salt and pepper means freshly ground black pepper. Oil refers to the olive oil you prefer to use unless cooking oil is specified and this refers to household vegetable oil.

BRAAI ★
AN INTRODUCTION

If you are human, you can braai. Cooking meat over a fire is something that defines our evolution as a species. Using fire, and braai tongs, is what separates us from other species. In South Africa it stands at the centre of our social interaction. Whether we are the descendants of hunters who walked the land in search of game, or the progeny of settlers who crossed the grasslands in search of hearth and home, making a braai is part of what defines us as South Africans.

Anything tastes better if you hold it over a fire for a while. Add the company of good friends or the embrace of your family, and even Brussels sprouts might taste good on the braai. That's why having a braai is such a quintessential part of being from here – we just love to get together, poke the fire a bit, chat about what's happening in the world and sit down to eat something delicious.

It's so much a part of who we are that many South Africans might be forgiven for believing we actually invented outdoor cooking. Well, of course we did, we even came up with a name for it (ignoring the obvious historical evidence of course). Americans cook hamburgers on outdoor gas cookers and call it barbecue. Argentinians may dress up like cowboys and hang around an *asado* waiting for their cow to cook. That's all very well, but every South African knows that cooking on a fire, outside, is called a braai.

We even dedicated a national holiday to the braai – Heritage Day, 24 September. We did it out of a sense of community, the burning desire for a day off work, and – as if we needed it – a proper reason to have a braai. It's a day when we coil the wors, mature the steaks, marinade the chops, get together and shout "Braai, the Beloved Country".

Jean Nel needs absolutely no encouragement, and very little excuse, to have a braai. He loves a braai so much he decided to make a living out of it. What better way for a kid from the Karoo countryside to earn himself a crust than by cooking for other people on an open fire, and even teaching his fellow South Africans how to braai? Fifteen years, and thousands of cooking fires, later he has assembled a collection of our classic braai recipes, as well as a few pearlers destined to become family favourites all over this great land.

FIRE
FUEL FOR THE BRAAI

Different braais do different things. The best braai in the world is the one you have with you when you want to cook something. Practically anything in which you can start and sustain a fire can be used to cook food on. There are the ever-popular kettle braais, ones made from 44-gallon drums, old gas cylinders, and so on. South Africans' ingenuity in fashioning something to make a fire in is limitless. It is much easier – and more practical here – to distinguish between the two main methods we use to cook over fire:

The Direct Method is where meat or ingredients sit on a grid directly over hot coals. The heat of the coals is applied directly to the food to sear and cook it.

The Indirect Method is where ingredients sit on a grid in a closed braai like a kettle. The heat of the coals is used to heat the interior of the kettle and cook anything in it.

So how do you make a fire? Anything combustible can be used to heat a can or a pot, or sear a steak, but some fuels are better than others. We choose wood or charcoal. Here's a certainty – you won't get it right first time. Cooking over coals is an art that takes time to learn. We invented the wheel millennia ago, and we still can't drive. What's to say we can cook just because we discovered fire?

The first thing to learn is to manage heat levels in your braai. Getting from a firelighter and a bag of charcoal to a bed of perfect glowing braai-ready coals requires practice. You want to cook over a hot bed of coals, not over flames. The emphasis here is on 'bed'. Don't skimp on the coal, there's nothing worse than running out of heat while your food is still cooking. Flames blacken your food and give it a sharp, sour taste.

Test a fire by holding your hand 2cm over the grid: 2 seconds for hot, 4 seconds for medium. Change hands each time you do this as your hand becomes used to the heat. Light a two-zone fire to control flare-ups and heat. The two-zone fire gives you somewhere to move your meat if the fat causes flames to flare or if it's too hot. The idea is to bank the coals so there is a slope to them from one side of the grid to the other. The fire will be hottest where the layer of coals is thickest, getting cooler as it thins out.

There are people who never make a braai without wood and they shout "Sissy!" at anyone who arrives with a bag of charcoal. But there's a really good case to be made for charcoal. It burns hottest and cleanest, and the braai is ready quicker than if you start with wood. The volume of wood you need to burn to get a usable bed of coals is massive compared to charcoal. Making charcoal is also a relatively easy-to-set-up industry that creates jobs, so we can all enjoy a braai in the Beloved Country.

Use a charcoal chimney. It looks like a fuss, but it's a good way to get the fire going quickly and well. It's also a way to get the fire going without firelighters. We don't want to preach against firelighters, but they are chemical accelerants and you have to consider what they might be doing to your food or your lungs. With a chimney, you just need some newspaper and a match. Reuse, Repair, Recycle.

Binne-braais, or indoor braais – those fancy built-in ones you get – have a fantastic system with a firebox where you can keep making coals as you cook. These can be added as you need them. If your braai is a kettle, or has no firebox, just start a second chimney burning when you start cooking – then you have fresh coals as you need them.

Briquettes are okay in a pinch – or in a kettle. They are made from sawdust, wood fragments and other flammable material. Often they are chemically treated. Increasingly there are briquettes available that are easier on the environment and on your food. They are free of harmful additives and get the job done perfectly.

If you must cook with wood, because it is beneath you to use new-fangled things like charcoal, here are a few pointers:

- Use the Boy Scout method and stack the wood in a little box. If you stack it in a teepee, it takes longer to become lit, and when you try to add more pieces, the coal bed will be uneven, causing new wood to roll off the pile.

- Use hard wood. Soft wood burns too quickly and does not produce a sustainable bed of coals.

- If you must burn wood, please burn alien species like black wattle. This will help people and organisations like Working for Water clear out the alien species that choke the waterways of the Beloved Country.

- Keeping a section of your fire for burning new wood and moving coals that are ready to the cooking area, using a spade or scraper, is a good idea for long braai sessions or large events.

- Never leave an open fire unattended, even for a minute, especially if alcohol and lots of people are involved. You have no idea how quickly a perfect cooking fire can become an inferno.

★ IN THE ★
FLAMES

Calamari is still a relatively inexpensive but delicious ingredient. Cook lots of it.

INGREDIENTS

400g large squid tubes

15ml olive oil

salt and pepper

lemon wedges to serve

MEXICAN SALSA

4 tomatoes, seeded
and diced (blocks)

1 red onion, finely chopped

1 avocado, sliced in blocks

100g corn kernels

1 red chilli, seeded and
finely chopped

1 garlic clove, crushed

30ml fresh coriander

75ml lemon juice

60ml olive oil

Combine all the salsa ingredients in a bowl and season. Transfer to your best platter.

Wash the calamari, and coat with olive oil. Heat a flat plate on the fire and cook until opaque. This should not take longer than 2 minutes. Please do not overcook!

Place calamari on top of Mexican salsa, drizzle with more oil if desired.

Serve hot with lemon wedges.

BRAAI NOTE: Calamari can also be braaied on wooden skewers. Soak skewers in cold water for 10 minutes first.

★ PRAWNS ★
WITH LEMON BUTTER AND PERI-PERI

Shellfish can take flavour so add chilli, lemon, garlic and spices in abundance.

INGREDIENTS

PERI-PERI

24 prawns, deveined

6 red chillies, chopped

1 clove garlic, finely chopped

5ml paprika

50ml white wine vinegar

125ml olive oil

30ml chopped flat-leaf parsley

lemon wedges to serve

LEMON BUTTER

24 prawns, deveined

60ml lemon juice

lemon rind from 1 lemon

125ml olive oil

100g soft butter

2 cloves garlic, finely chopped

15ml chopped flat-leaf parsley

5ml finely chopped rosemary and thyme

salt and pepper

PERI-PERI

Add chillies (remove seeds for a less fiery peri-peri), garlic, paprika, white wine vinegar, olive oil and parsley in a small pot and simmer for 3 minutes. Cool slightly and blend in a food processor until smooth. Cool completely. Place in a small bowl, alongside the braai.

Toss deveined prawns with 45ml sauce. Throw prawns on an oiled grid and braai for 2–3 minutes per side, turning. Brush with any remaining peri-peri sauce.

BRAAI NOTE: Leftover peri-peri sauce will last up to a month, refrigerated.

LEMON BUTTER

In a small pot, add lemon juice, rind, olive oil, butter, garlic, fresh herbs and seasoning. Simmer for 2 minutes until the butter is melted.

Toss prawns with the lemon and herb butter. Throw on the braai and braai 2–3 minutes per side, turning. Brush with remaining lemon butter.

KITCHEN TIP: Marinate prawns with your choice of basting sauce in a Ziploc bag, refrigerated for 1 hour maximum.

BRAAIED HALOUMI
AND LEMON SALAD

Haloumi cheese can take high heat so it's perfect for the braai. Braai the lemons... it intensifies the flavour.

INGREDIENTS

30ml harissa paste

30ml olive oil, plus extra to serve with the haloumi

400g haloumi, sliced into 1cm thickness

3 lemons, halved

60g black olives, pitted

125g baby tomatoes, halved

mint leaves

250g rocket

salt and freshly ground black pepper

Marinate the haloumi slices in the harissa and olive oil.

Braai the haloumi slices on a direct, medium heat for 2–3 minutes.

Braai lines will form on the surface of the cheese.

Rub the cut side of the lemons into the remaining harissa oil.

Braai skin-side down for 3 minutes.

Transfer haloumi cheese to a platter with the braaied lemons, rocket, mint, olives and baby tomatoes.

Squeeze the lemons over the salad.

BRAAIED TUNA ON CROSTINI

Tuna should be grilled on a high heat to char the outside but leave it raw in the middle. This only takes 2 to 3 minutes, but leave it a touch longer if you like it cooked through.

INGREDIENTS

500g fresh tuna

olive oil

salt and freshly ground black pepper

fresh rocket

45ml white wine

150g soft butter, diced

30ml lemon juice

salt and freshly ground black pepper

crostini (ciabatta)

Place white wine in a small saucepot over a medium heat. Add butter piece by piece. Add lemon juice and seasoning once butter has melted. Put in a little bowl.

Infuse 2 cloves fresh garlic with olive oil in a little bowl. Set aside.

Brush tuna with olive oil and season with salt and freshly ground black pepper.

Cook in a cast iron pan directly over the flames for 1 minute per side or to your liking.

Rest tuna for a few minutes. While tuna is resting, slice crostini (ciabatta). Rub with the whole garlic cloves and braai. Crostini should have grid lines but not be toasted.

Place crostini on a platter, top with rocket and place sliced tuna on top.

BRAAIED ASPARAGUS
WITH SHAVED PARMESAN

I love the woody flavour from the braaied stems.

INGREDIENTS

600g asparagus, trimmed

45ml olive oil

6 spring onions

15ml chopped thyme

10 basil leaves, torn

salt and freshly ground
black pepper

Combine the olive oil, spring onions, thyme and basil leaves and seasoning.

Remove the tough ends from the asparagus spears. Blanch asparagus and spring onions in boiling water for 1 minute. Drain and refresh in iced water. Dry asparagus and spring onion. Place in a dish.

Pour olive oil–herb marinade on asparagus and spring onions. Allow to marinate for 30 minutes or more.

Braai asparagus and spring onions for 5 to 6 minutes, turning occasionally. Serve with shaved parmesan.

CHICKEN WINGS ★ 2 WAYS ★
STICKY; LEMON AND LIME

Delicious hot or cold, and children love gnawing on these wings too.

INGREDIENTS

STICKY CHICKEN WINGS

1kg chicken wings

30ml honey

30ml sherry

30ml tomato sauce

30ml soy sauce

30ml lemon juice

30ml olive oil

1 x 4cm fresh ginger, grated

2 cloves garlic, crushed

90ml water

LEMON AND LIME CHICKEN WINGS

1kg chicken wings

60ml lemon juice

60ml lime juice

2 small red chillies, finely diced

15ml castor sugar

sea salt and freshly ground black pepper

45ml olive oil

STICKY CHICKEN WINGS

Combine the sticky marinade. Whisk.

Remove the wing tips from the chicken wings and place it in an ovenproof glass dish. Allow to marinate for 1 hour. Place chicken and sticky marinade in a pot and simmer for 10 minutes.

Braai over medium-hot coals for about 20 minutes until brown and sticky. Keep brushing with marinade.

LEMON AND LIME CHICKEN WINGS

Combine the marinade.

Remove the wing tips from the chicken wings and place in a glass dish. Marinate for 1 hour.

Braai over medium-hot coals for 20 minutes, basting with remaining marinade.

BRAAI NOTE: Try the lemon and lime marinade over lamb chops or prawns.

EXOTIC MUSHROOM SKEWERS

Cultivated for centuries in the Far East and now increasingly available from all over. Choose exotic mushrooms that look plump and firm.

INGREDIENTS

500g exotic mushrooms
(Portobello, button, shitake and King Oyster work best)

125ml olive oil

15ml mixed dried herbs

salt and freshly ground black pepper

Slice Portobello in half, leave button whole, slice shitake in halves and keep King Oysters whole. Skewer on metal skewers. Mix olive oil, mixed dried herbs, salt and freshly ground black pepper in a bowl. Braai exotic mushroom kebabs on direct heat for 4 to 5 minutes per side.

RARE RUMP SLICED
WITH SALT AND LEMON JUICE

Rump steak may not be as tender as other steak cuts but it's a full-flavoured meat, perfect for the braai.

INGREDIENTS

400g rump steak, trimmed

30ml olive oil

15ml oregano leaves

15ml thyme leaves

5ml rosemary leaves

freshly ground black pepper

2 lemons

sea salt

Marinate rump in olive oil, herbs and freshly ground black pepper.

Place rump on an oiled grid and braai for 6 minutes, rotating once. Turn over and braai for a further 4 minutes. Scatter salt liberally on a wooden chopping board. Place the rump on the salt. Squeeze juice from 1 lemon all over the rump, then slice. Squeeze the remaining lemon over the slices to taste, then serve.

LEMONY HAKE ★ PARCELS ★ ON THE BRAAI

Be careful when you unwrap the foil after the hake is done. There will be a release of very hot steam. Let it rest first.

INGREDIENTS

HAKE

4 x 200g fillets of hake, skin on and boned

90ml olive oil

1 clove garlic, chopped

juice and zest of 1 lemon

fresh chopped herbs of your choice – dill, basil or flat-leaf parsley work well

4 x A4 size foil

LEMON CHILLI MAYONNAISE

1 egg yolk

10ml Dijon mustard

10ml lemon juice

200ml olive oil

15ml grated lemon zest

5ml paprika

salt and freshly ground black pepper

HAKE

Mix olive oil, garlic, lemon juice and zest in a small bowl. Add fresh chopped herbs.

Divide the olive oil in 4 portions and pour onto the foil. Put a fillet of hake on top. Scatter with lemon juice, lemon zest and garlic. Fold in an envelope shape. Put on a direct hot braai. Braai for 4 to 5 minutes. Remove from the braai but don't open as the envelopes will have lots of steam that needs to cool down.

LEMON CHILLI MAYONNAISE

Place the egg yolk, mustard and lemon juice in a blender and process to combine. With the motor running, add olive oil in a slow, steady stream until mixture begins to emulsify and the mayonnaise begins to thicken. Stir in the lemon zest, paprika and seasoning.

KITCHEN NOTE: Store-bought mayonnaise may be used instead of making your own.

BRAAI GHANOUSH
★ WITH BABY TOMATO STICKS ★

You will never use a conventional oven once you've braaied aubergine; the smokiness is magic.

INGREDIENTS

AUBERGINE

2 large aubergine

10ml salt

juice of half a lemon

2 garlic cloves, crushed

60ml olive oil

15ml chopped flat-leaf parsley, plus extra to serve

pita breads

TOMATO STICKS

400g baby tomatoes

4 cloves garlic, thinly sliced

fresh bay leaves

60ml olive oil

AUBERGINE

Prick the aubergine with a fork. Braai for 10 to15 minutes, turning often until tender. Remove and cool. Peel aubergine skin once cool enough to handle, discard skin. Place the flesh in a sieve over a bowl and drain. Put the aubergine in a food processor with the salt, lemon juice, garlic, parsley and olive oil. Purée. Pour into a bowl, drizzle with extra olive oil. Serve with baby tomato sticks and braaied pita bread.

BRAAI NOTE: Use a mortar and pestle for a coarser texture to make Braai Ghanoush.

TOMATO STICKS

Skewer baby tomatoes, garlic and bay leaves onto wooden skewers. Brush with oil.

Braai for 4 to 5 minutes, turning regularly. Baby tomatoes should be blistered.

CHORIZO
★ WITH SHERRY ★

One of my all-time favourites,
so quick and easy.

INGREDIENTS

500g smoked chorizo
15ml olive oil
60ml sherry
1 baguette bread, sliced

Toss the chorizo with the olive oil and sherry. Braai on a high heat for 2 to 3 minutes. Chorizo should be crispy.

Slice chorizo on an angle and pour more sherry over if desired.

Serve with sliced baguette.

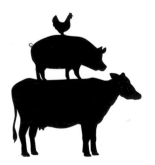

CHICKEN ★TAPAS★

The spices here are pure Spanish and need a glass of sherry to help them down.

INGREDIENTS

500g cubed (2.5cm)
chicken breast

5ml each fennel seeds, cumin
and coriander seeds

5ml smoked paprika

30ml dried oregano

lemon juice

3 cloves garlic, crushed

1 bay leaf for marinade and a
few more to skewer with the
chicken tapas

45ml red wine vinegar

45ml olive oil

salt and freshly ground
black pepper

Soak wooden skewers in cold water for 10 minutes.

Put the fennel, cumin and coriander seeds into a small frying pan. Dry-fry for a few seconds, shaking the pan from side to side. The aroma should fill your kitchen. Crush seeds with a mortar and pestle. Add all the other ingredients, stir well. Add to cubed chicken. Cover and refrigerate.

Thread the chicken onto soaked skewers with whole bay leaves on every odd one. Braai over direct heat for 9 to 10 minutes, turning once.

DIRECT
COOKING

LEMON AND HERB ★ CHICKEN KEBAB

The pick-up stick is one of our most favourite braai snacks. A braai gets a new chic look with a range of tasty sticks!

INGREDIENTS

MARINADE

2 lemons, halved

60ml olive oil

2 fresh rosemary sprigs, roughly chopped

4 fresh thyme sprigs, leaves picked

4 fresh marjoram sprigs, leaves picked

1 garlic clove, crushed

freshly ground black pepper

Wooden skewers

Soak wooden skewers in cold water for 10 minutes.

Juice the lemons. Cut each lemon in half and in half again. Place all the ingredients in a Ziploc bag. Add 6 chicken fillets to the bag and marinate for 1 hour.

Bring the chicken to room temperature and slice into cubes. Cut meat in 1.5cm cubes, otherwise it will take too long to braai. Thread the chicken onto the soaked bamboo skewers. Allow 100g chicken per kebab.

One of the secrets of a good kebab is not to pack the skewers too tightly. Leave some gaps around the meat so it can braai through thoroughly.

Braai over a medium-hot direct fire for 6 to 8 minutes on each side. Baste with the leftover marinade.

Ziploc plastic bags come in handy when marinating meat pieces. Simply add the marinade to the meat, seal it and refrigerate until needed. When marinating with lemon juice you have to be careful, as lemon juice will cook the meat.

★ MOZAMBIQUE PERI-PERI ★
CHICKEN FLATTY

Get one whole bird out... but it's only the beginning. The peri-peri goes on anything... so get the prawns, chicken and meat ready. Baste and braai it!

INGREDIENTS

1 whole chicken

10 red chillies

4 cloves garlic

60ml white wine vinegar

125ml olive oil

3 lemons

Roughly chop the chillies with the seeds. Place them in a blender with the peeled garlic. Blend. With the motor running, add the vinegar through the opening of the blender. Pour in the olive oil slow and steady. The mixture should have a creamy look. Blend for no longer than 4 minutes. Bottle sauce.

Spatchcock the chicken with a cook's knife. Cut through the spine. Open the chicken. Lay it out on a chopping board, then bash the breast with the heel of your hand. You now have a chicken flatty. Transfer chicken to a dish. Pour peri-peri sauce over it. Coat the chicken all over with the marinade. Leave to marinate for 2 hours.

Braai on medium coals, skin-side up for 20 minutes. Turn and braai skin-side down for 15 minutes. You may need to turn your flatty for 5 minutes or more depending on how big the bird is.

Serve with potato wedges (page 110).

BEEF/OSTRICH
★ **BURGER** ★
WITH ALL THE TRIMMINGS

Burgers are one of the most popular foods around the world, but so many of them are so utterly dismal. When you make your own burger you have control over what goes into your mince. So head off to the kitchen and make your own.

INGREDIENTS

FOR THE BURGER

1kg lean beef mince
1 onion, finely diced
2 cloves garlic, finely chopped
30ml dried herbs
30ml chopped Italian parsley
salt and freshly ground
black pepper
vegetable oil for brushing

Place the onions, mince, garlic, dried herbs and parsley, salt and pepper in a bowl and mix well. Squeeze the mince through your fingers until well combined. Divide the meat into 6 equal balls. The burgers should be 2cm thick (not a bulging burger). Cover with cling film and refrigerate. Take burgers out of the fridge, let them lose their chill a bit, then brush with oil.

Braai burgers on a medium-high heat. Braai for 3 minutes on each side. Do not turn burgers. If you like a well-done burger, braai for another minute. Braai bacon at the same time. This should not take longer than 1½ minutes each side.

Place sliced cheese on your burgers.

Lightly braai the opened rolls. Don't burn them! Spread rolls with Dijon mustard and mayonnaise.

Fill the rolls with the cheesy-melted burgers. Build burgers with whatever you desire.

BRAAI NOTE: You can replace the beef mince with 1kg ostrich mince.

★ CAJUN BEEF ★

Cajun-Creole beef with garlic mayonnaise. An all-time favourite at The Good Food Studio.

INGREDIENTS

1 small beef fillet, 700–800g

CAJUN-CREOLE RUB

5ml each dried thyme, dried oregano, basil, black peppercorns, white peppercorns, onion powder, garlic powder, salt and cumin seeds

10ml paprika

Put all the ingredients into a mortar and grind with pestle.

Rub the spice paste onto the beef fillet and massage the meat with 30ml olive oil. Set aside, wrap and marinate for 1 hour.

Make the garlic mayonnaise: Rub the papery peels off the heads of garlic and trim the tips of the garlic. The garlic cloves should be exposed. Wrap in foil and braai for 25 to 30 minutes. Press the garlic purée from the roasted garlic and add to mayonnaise.

Place the fillet on an oiled grid with a drip tray underneath. Braai for 25 to 35 minutes.

BRAAIED, MARINATED ★ BEEF FILLET ★

My corporate team buildings will be lost without this. By far the easiest recipe! Try it!

INGREDIENTS

1.2kg beef fillet

sprigs of young rosemary

2 sprigs marjoram/ oregano leaves

60ml balsamic vinegar

wholegrain mustard

coarse sea salt

freshly ground black pepper

water-soaked cotton string

Smear the beef fillet with the wholegrain mustard and tie with water-soaked cotton string. Thread sprigs of rosemary and other herbs through the string. Sear the beef fillet over a very warm direct fire and season with coarse salt and freshly ground black pepper. Scatter the beef fillet with balsamic vinegar. Return to a medium heat until cooked.

BRAAI NOTE: Fillet is the prime beef cut with little visible fat, it's so tender. I braai my fillet on an oiled braai grid for 10 minutes, rotating once. Turn over and braai for a further 6 minutes, rotating once again. Rest for 5 minutes before slicing.

BRAAIED T-BONE
★ WITH MONKEY GLAND SAUCE ★

A Braai the Beloved Country sauce, so South African. What's this sauce without our iconic Mrs Ball's chutney? Monkey gland sauce goes well with any burger. This sauce stores well for up to 3 days.

INGREDIENTS

T-bone steaks – 500g or more in weight

rosemary branches

olive oil

salt and freshly ground black pepper

MONKEY GLAND SAUCE

1 onion, finely chopped

5ml garlic, crushed

5ml Tabasco

125ml cup water

1 x 400g chopped tin tomatoes

250ml tomato sauce

125ml Worcestershire sauce

250ml Mrs Ball's chutney

30ml white wine vinegar

T-BONE STEAK

Marinate the T-bone by putting a rosemary branch on a plate, top with the T-bone, then cover with the remaining rosemary branches. Cover with plastic wrap while you make the monkey gland sauce.

MONKEY GLAND SAUCE

In a pot, simmer onions and garlic over medium heat until soft. Add the rest of the ingredients, stir to combine and heat through. Reduce heat to low and simmer for 35 to 40 minutes.

Remove the T-bone steak from the rosemary branch marinade. Reserve the rosemary. Season with salt and freshly ground black pepper. Brush with olive oil.

Braai the T-bone on an oiled grid over a high direct heat: 5 minutes on each side for medium-rare or braai to your liking. Moisten occasionally with rosemary.

Serve with the monkey gland sauce.

★ SIMPLE BRAAIED ★ LAMB CHOP

There is nothing as satisfying as simple yet perfectly braaied lamb cutlets.

INGREDIENTS

4 lamb cutlets

60ml olive oil

15ml each salt and freshly ground black pepper

Rub the lamb cutlets with olive oil, salt and freshly ground black pepper.

Place lamb on oiled braai grid and braai for 3 to 4 minutes, rotating once.

Rest for 5 minutes before serving.

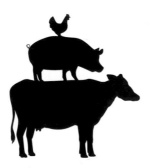

The best cut for kebabs is from the leg of the lamb. It's more tender than the shoulder part.

INGREDIENTS

LAMB

2kg deboned lamb, cubed 2.5cm or close

metal skewers

CURRY SAUCE

30ml olive oil

15ml butter

2 onions, finely chopped

3 cloves garlic, crushed

1 x 5cm fresh ginger, peeled and grated

30ml curry powder

5ml turmeric

5ml sugar

250ml vinegar

250ml Mrs Ball's fruit chutney

125ml sherry

salt and freshly ground black pepper

6 bay leaves

15–20 lemon leaves

Heat the butter and oil in a pan. Fry the onions until softened. Stir in the garlic, ginger, curry powder, turmeric and sugar for a minute. Add vinegar, chutney and sherry and bring to the boil. Season. Take off the heat and cool down to room temperature.

Place the cubed lamb in a bowl, add the curry marinate and coat evenly. Add the bay leaves, cover and marinate for 6 to 24 hours, stirring once or twice.

Thread lamb cubes and lemon leaves on metal skewers. Don't discard marinade. Clamp all the sosaties on a closed hinged grid. Braai for 10 minutes over hot coals, turning once.

Bring the remaining marinade to the boil, stirring. Place in a bowl and serve on a wooden board with the sosaties.

★ PORK RIBS ★
START IN THE KITCHEN, FINISH ON DIRECT FIRE

Another Good Food Studio staple recipe. These ribs dance between your oven and the fire. They take a little time but are so delicious.

INGREDIENTS

PORK RIBS

1.5kg pork spare ribs

1 cinnamon stick

2 star anise

STICKY MARINADE

60ml dark soy sauce

30ml black bean sauce

30ml sweet chilli sauce

200ml fresh orange juice

15ml grated ginger

15ml brown sugar

Preheat the oven to 180°C. Lay the ribs in a large roasting tin, cover with enough hot water. Add the cinnamon stick and star anise. Bake for 40 minutes. Do not boil the ribs. Set aside once cooked in the oven.

Mix together all the ingredients for the sticky marinade. Simmer marinade in a small pot for a few minutes. Pour sticky marinade over ribs. Leave to stand for 15 minutes, turning the ribs twice. Braai the ribs over a low-medium heat for 15 minutes. Turn the ribs after 10 minutes and baste with more marinade. Make sure ribs are cooked through.

★ CHAR SIU ★ PORK FILLET LETTUCE ROLLS

Let's braai something straight out of Chinatown. It's easy! All you need are a few Chinese grocery items. They last forever in the grocery cupboard.

INGREDIENTS

2 pork fillets (400 to 450g each)

15ml 5 spice powder

45ml honey

45ml soy sauce

45ml hoi sin sauce

1 x 5cm fresh ginger, peeled

1 clove garlic, crushed

Ready bought plum sauce

TO MAKE LETTUCE ROLLS

1 large iceberg lettuce, broken into leaves

½ cucumber

6 spring onions, trimmed

fresh coriander leaves

Grate the ginger and squeeze out the juice in a non-metallic dish. Add the rest of the ingredients and stir. Trim any excess fat and membrane from the pork fillet. Add to the marinade, coat and marinate for a maximum of 2 hours (due to the high salt content – we don't want any tough pork fillet).

Cut the cucumber in half lengthwise, scoop out the seeds and slice into long strips. Cut the spring onions lengthwise into thin strips. Arrange on a platter with the iceberg lettuce and some plum sauce.

Remove the pork fillet from the marinade 30 minutes before you want to braai it. Braai on an oiled grid over medium-high heat for 12 to 15 minutes, basting with the leftover marinade every 3 to 4 minutes.

The fillet will shrink a little and have the most incredible reddish brown colour. Transfer to a wooden board and let it rest for 5 minutes. Carve into very thin slices. Put it on the platter with the vegetables and plum sauce. Instruct your guests to make their own rolls with a lettuce leaf, a slice of pork fillet, cucumber, spring onion, coriander and sauce.

Cos or butter lettuce is great with the rolls too.

★ WORS ROLL ★
AND BOOZY ONIONS

I believe you can buy good quality sausages much more easily than trying to make your own. Track down a good butcher. Braai the sausages last, on a low temperature — you don't want the skin to burst!

INGREDIENTS

BOOZY ONIONS

6 white onions, thinly sliced

1 can beer

200ml brown sugar

60ml cup balsamic vinegar

125ml cup water

WORS ROLLS

12 boerewors (weight approximately 110g per sausage)

12 good quality hotdog rolls

wholegrain mustard mixed with mayo to spread on the rolls

rocket (optional)

Place onion, beer, sugar, balsamic vinegar, olive oil and water in a saucepan. Bring to a high simmer, then reduce. Simmer at a lower heat for about 40 minutes, stirring occasionally. This will prevent the onions from sticking on the base.

Braai sausages, turning for 6 to 8 minutes or until cooked through.

Warm the hotdog rolls, cut in the middle but without slicing through the roll. Fill the rolls with the wholegrain mustard mayonnaise, rocket and boerewors, and top with the boozy onions.

BRAAI NOTE: Make the boozy onions in a small pot on the colder side of the fire.

★ HERB AND GARLIC ★ SAUSAGE COIL

Get your hinged grid out. A great way to feed lots of people without turning individual sausages. Ask your butcher to make you one long untwisted sausage. You'll need metal skewers for this. The secret of juicy sausage is to braai it slowly over a low heat.

INGREDIENTS

1.6kg sausage coil

2 lemons

2 bay leaves, torn

15ml fresh rosemary leaves, chopped

15ml fresh thyme leaves

30ml chopped Italian parsley

8 sage leaves

3 cloves garlic, sliced

salt and freshly ground black pepper

30ml olive oil

Coil the sausage into a long tight spiral. Place two large metal skewers at right angles through the sausage to secure it.

Peel lemon rind with a vegetable peeler and slice into thin strips. Combine the lemon rind, fresh herbs and oil into a small bowl. Squeeze half a lemon out into the herb–olive oil mixture. Sprinkle the coil with the mixture. Reserve some mixture for later. Braai coil over medium-low heat until brown underneath, then turn it over. Sprinkle with remaining herb–oil mixture. Braai until sausage is cooked through.

★ NO CASING ★ SAUSAGES

These handmade, hand-rolled sausages made by you are about sharing. Serve with beetroot relish, tzatziki, olives and braai some pita breads...

INGREDIENTS

HANDMADE SPICED LAMB SAUSAGES

500g lamb mince

2 cloves garlic, minced

5ml ground cumin

5ml dried mint

5ml paprika

5ml dried oregano

3ml nutmeg

3ml cinnamon

3ml ground coriander

100ml water

salt and freshly ground black pepper

lemon wedges to serve

TZATZIKI

350g natural yoghurt

1 garlic clove, crushed

½ cucumber, grated and strained

pinch of dried mint

salt and freshly ground black pepper

Combine all the sausage ingredients together, holding back some water until the moisture is moist but not too sticky. Season to taste, mix well. Wet your hands. Shape into 16 sausages. Braai on an oiled flat plate over medium, direct heat for 3 to 4 minutes until golden and cooked through. Season again, drizzle with olive oil and chopped coriander (optional).

Serve with lemon wedges.

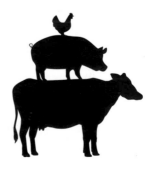

★ VENISON LOIN ★
WITH MOSKONFYT SAUCE

In a country known for the variety and affordability of its venison, we eat surprisingly little of it. Help me change this.

INGREDIENTS

1 venison loin fillet, trimmed

MOSKONFYT SAUCE
juice of 2 oranges
45ml moskonfyt
60ml olive oil
125ml red wine
5ml ground coriander
15ml HP sauce

Mix the sauce ingredients in a bowl and marinate 4 to 5 cm slices of the venison loin in the moskonfyt sauce in the fridge overnight, or for at least 4 hours.

Strain off the sauce just before you braai, as you don't want excess marinade to smother the coals. Braai on an oiled grid for 25 to 30 minutes.

RUMP SOSATIE
★ CHIMMICHURRI ★

Absolutely addictive, chimmichurri sauce from Argentina is the perfect match for beef. You want the kebabs seared on the outside and medium-rare in the middle.

INGREDIENTS

1kg rump cubes

1 lemon, cut in half

CHIMMICHURRI

2 garlic cloves, coarsely chopped

5ml salt

30g Italian parsley, coarsely chopped

30g coriander, coarsely chopped

5ml cayenne pepper

5ml paprika

60ml olive oil

30ml red wine vinegar

Put the garlic and salt in a mortar and pound to a coarse paste. Add the herbs, spices and olive oil. Pound to combine. Add the vinegar. Set aside for the flavours to develop.

Put rump cubes in a non-metallic dish or in a Ziploc bag. Pour chimmichurri over and toss to coat. Marinate for 1 hour. The vinegar may start to cook the meat. Remove from the dish or bag 20 minutes prior to braaing and arrange on a metal skewer.

On a direct hot heat, braai rump kebabs for 4 to 5 minutes per side. Remove and squeeze fresh lemon over.

★ CABERNET SAUVIGNON ★
BEEF RIB EYE

Get your best quality Cabernet Sauvignon out for this very simple recipe...

INGREDIENTS

4 x 400–450g beef rib eye

600ml good quality cabernet sauvignon (drink the rest)

1 bulb garlic, cloves separated, tips exposed (cut it off with a sharp knife), lightly crushed

5ml dried thyme

5ml freshly ground black pepper

Put the rib eye in a non-metallic dish and pour the red wine over it. Add the other ingredients. Make sure the rib eyes don't overlap. Cover and refrigerate overnight. Turn twice. Remove the rib eye from the fridge half an hour before braaing, and take it out of the marinade. Brush with olive oil and season with salt. Braai rib eye on an oiled grid over a very hot, direct heat for 5 minutes per side. Turn once more for 1 to 2 minutes.

Let rib eye rest for 10 minutes.

WEST COAST ★ SNOEK ★

This is a recipe from a fisherman in the Paternoster area. No one can braai snoek like people from the West Coast...

BRAAIED WEST COAST SNOEK WITH APRICOT JAM

A clean hinged grid, a metal spatula and non-stick spray is needed for this one!

1 side of West Coast snoek

GLAZE

60g butter

45ml oil

1 clove garlic, crushed

30ml apricot jam

15ml sweet chilli sauce

45ml lemon juice

freshly ground black pepper

Combine glaze ingredients in a small pot, heat and stir until combined and smooth.

Place snoek on an oiled hinged braai grid, skin-side down. Braai for 20 minutes skin-side down and turn for the last 5 minutes.

The snoek should come off the grid easily, using the metal spatula.

BRAAIED BUTTERFLIED FISH

This is fantastic for snoek, but will work perfectly for any linefish you may prefer. Use a non-stick cooking spray for your hinged braai grid.

INGREDIENTS

1 whole fish (1.5kg – 2kg) cleaned and butterflied

MARINADE
60ml vinegar

30ml mustard powder

5ml paprika

2 cloves garlic, crushed

250ml olive oil

60ml lemon juice

chopped fresh herbs – basil, flat-leaf parsley and dill

salt and freshly ground black pepper

In a small bowl, mix all ingredients together.

Place butterflied fish on an oiled hinged grid. Season with salt and pepper.

Braai on hot coals for between 20 and 25 minutes or until the skin is crisp and the flesh is just cooked.

Remove to a large platter and pour marinade over it.

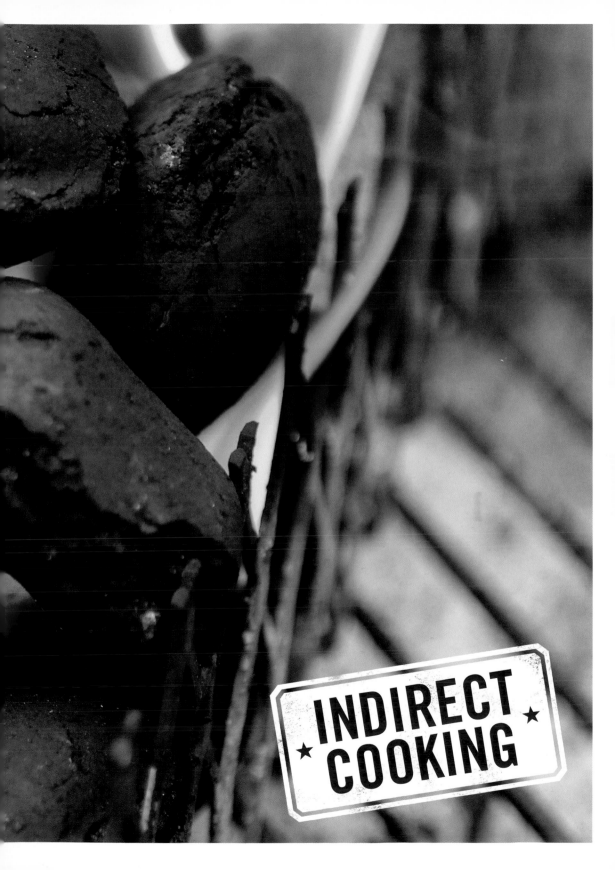

INDIRECT
★ COOKING

★ PORK BELLY ★
WITH APRICOT JAM GLAZE

Crispy, succulent and completely heavenly.

INGREDIENTS

1 x 2kg pork belly rind, scored
apricot jam
lemon juice

Ask your butcher to score the rind or score it with a sharp knife, then moisten it with a little olive oil and rub it thoroughly with salt.

Set aside for a good few hours.

Just before braaing, rub the pork belly lightly again with olive oil. Place on an oiled grid and braai for 1 to 1½ hours. Pork should be just cooked (braaied through), so if you're unsure, insert a skewer into the thickest part of the meat. The juices should run clear.

15 minutes before the end of braaing the pork belly, brush some apricot jam mixed with lemon juice over the rind.

BRAAI NOTE: Add fennel seeds as an alternative with the salt when rubbing the rind.

If you are not a fan of apricot jam, use quince jam, marmalade or sweet chilli sauce to brown the pork belly.

★ ROAST PORK LOIN ★
WITH CINNAMON-SPIKED APPLES

INGREDIENTS

900g – 1kg pork loin,
skin on

10ml salt

5ml fennel seeds

5ml caraway seeds

4 red apples

4 cinnamon sticks

REDCURRANT SAUCE

250ml store-bought
redcurrant jelly

250ml chicken stock

375ml sparkling rosé

Score the skin of the pork, cutting through to the flesh.

Put the salt, fennel and caraway seeds in a mortar and pound till crushed. Rub the mixture into the cuts of the pork. Set aside. Score the apples around the middle with a sharp knife. Push cinnamon sticks into the centre of the apples.

Place pork loin on a well-oiled grid, close the lid and braai for 30 minutes. The skin should start to crisp up. Arrange the cinnamon apples around the pork. Close the lid and braai for 40 minutes.

For a crispier skin, braai for another 10 to 15 minutes. Skin should be crisp and golden in colour. Allow the pork to rest for 10 to 15 minutes.

To make the redcurrant sauce, place the jelly, rosé and stock in a small pot. Stir to dissolve jelly and bring to the boil. Reduce heat and simmer for 15 minutes until slightly thickened.

★ CAN CAN ★
CHICKENS

Beer keeps the meat moist during cooking and adds a wonderful flavour. The bird is crispy on the outside and succulent on the inside.

INGREDIENTS

1 lemon, halved

45ml dried herbs

5ml salt

5ml freshly ground
black pepper

15ml olive oil

1.5kg whole chicken,
giblets removed

1 x 340ml can beer

Squeeze half a lemon into a small bowl and add the dried herbs, salt and pepper and olive oil. Rub the dried herb mixture onto the inside and outside of the chicken. Insert the fresh herbs and the other half of the lemon into the cavity of the chicken.

Drink a third of the beer. Place the chicken over the can of beer. The chicken should sit upright and the drumsticks should point downwards.

Balance the can and the chicken on top of the braai grid over the middle section of the fire. Make sure the drip tray is underneath the chicken.

Cover with the lid and braai without opening for 75 minutes. The juices should run clear when the thigh is pierced with a sharp knife. The chicken should have a beautiful braaied look. Remove from the braai, discard the beer can and allow the chicken to rest for 10 minutes before serving.

BRAAI NOTE: Ready-bought sauces: Because of the sugar content, these sauces are meant to be used at the tail end to caramelise any meats.

TANDOORI CHICKEN

Exotic spices, natural yoghurt, a braai: do we need to say more?

INGREDIENTS

1.5kg chicken, spatchcocked

150ml natural Greek yoghurt

10ml coriander seeds

5ml cumin seeds

45ml lemon juice

finely grated zest of 1 lemon

1 x 5cm fresh ginger, peeled, chopped

2 cloves

1ml chilli powder

45ml vegetable oil

5ml paprika

5ml garam masala

salt and freshly ground black pepper

Place a frying pan over low heat and dry-roast the coriander seeds until aromatic.

In the same pan, dry-roast the cumin seeds until aromatic.

Grind the seeds to a fine powder using a mortar and pestle.

Combine all the remaining ingredients.

Using a sharp knife, make a number of incisions in the chicken skin (2.5cm).

Spread the mixture all over the chicken.

Cover and marinate overnight in the refrigerator.

Bring chicken to room temperature 30 minutes before braaing.

Place chicken on an oiled grid.

Cover and cook for 1 hour or until braaied through. Baste with the remaining marinade twice during the braai time.

STUFFED GREEK CHICKEN

A couple of my favourite ingredients... chicken breast with skin on and feta cheese... to make an easy mid-week meal.

INGREDIENTS

4 chicken breasts with wings attached and skin on

GREEK FETA AND HERB STUFFING

250g feta, crumbled

2 handfuls basil, mint and flat-leaf parsley, chopped

5 cloves garlic, crushed

100g depitted black olives

salt and freshly ground black pepper

90ml olive oil

2 lemons sliced thickly in rings

soaked string

tin foil container

Combine the stuffing ingredients in a small bowl.

Push stuffing under the chicken breast skin. Rub the skin with a little olive oil and season. For a more lemon zing, tie lemon slices in place with string that has been soaked in water.

Place the chicken in a tin foil container and braai for 40 to 45 minutes.

BRAAI NOTE: A covered braai shortens the cooking time of meat by up to 25 per cent and enhances the smoky flavour.

WHOLE FISH
★ THAI STYLE ★

A whole fish adds drama to the table; it's about sharing and bringing friends together, as long they don't mind getting their fingers sticky.

INGREDIENTS

1 x 1.5kg line fish

1 trimmed lemongrass, cut into 5cm lengths

4 garlic cloves, bruised

2 limes (or lemons) thinly sliced

salt and freshly ground black pepper

THAI DRESSING

125ml sweet chilli sauce

60ml soy sauce

125ml lime juice (or lemon juice)

5ml castor sugar

1 x 5cm fresh ginger, finely grated

5ml fish sauce (nam pla)

45ml peanut sauce

Ask your fishmonger to clean and scale the fish. When braaing a whole fish, the flesh will continue to cook for a while after it's been removed from the braai, so be aware of overcooking.

Rinse fish inside and out under cold running water. Pat dry with paper towel. Using a sharp knife, score the fish on the diagonal 3 or 4 times on each side through the skin, about 1.5cm into the flesh.

Place a large sheet of baking paper on top of a large sheet of heavy-duty foil. Place fish in centre of paper. Fill the cavity with lemongrass, garlic, limes and salt and pepper.

Fold the baking paper and foil to enclose fish. Braai the fish for 30 to 35 minutes. Turn halfway, or until cooked through. Let the fish rest for 10 minutes after it is taken off the braai.

Combine all ingredients in a bowl and stir well.

Unwrap fish and transfer to a serving platter. Drizzle with the dressing. Top with coriander sprigs and spring onions.

BRAAI TIP: When selecting fish, look for bright clear eyes, not sunken and sad eyes, as that will show you the freshness of the fish.

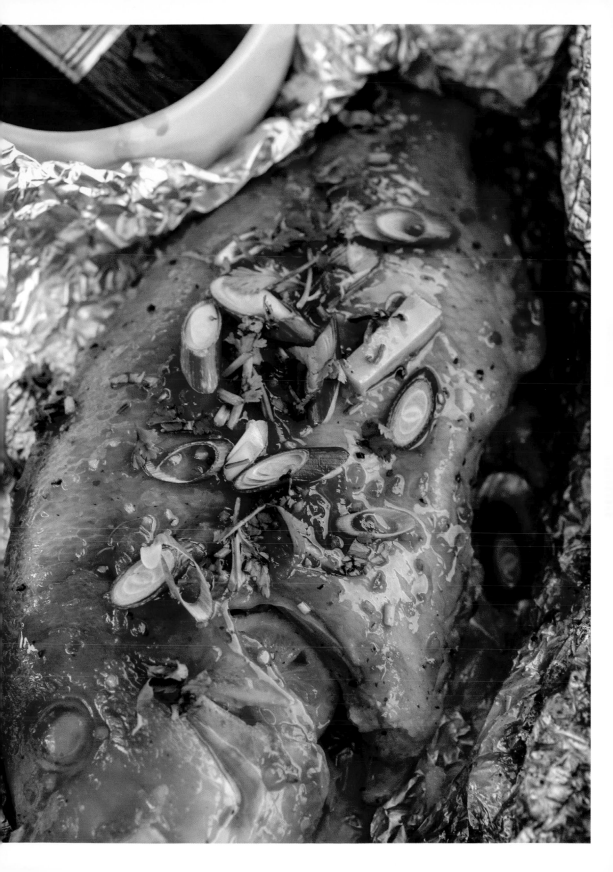

SALMON ON A PLANK

A very easy but delicious way to prepare Norwegian salmon. This is one braai dish that your guests will go wow about. You can use the plank technique for chicken and beef fillet too.

INGREDIENTS

1 whole side of salmon

salt and freshly ground black pepper

30ml olive oil

smoking chips

CRÈME FRAÎCHE DRESSING

250ml crème fraîche

45ml lemon juice

30ml spring onion, chopped

15ml chopped capers (or caper berries)

salt and pepper

Mix all ingredients in a bowl.

Rub some olive oil on one side of an untreated plank which has been soaked in water, wine or beer for 1 hour. Place the salmon on it, skin-side down. Season with salt and pepper and brush with olive oil. Add the smoking chips to the coals (you should soak these for 1 hour in water too). Close the lid and braai for 25 minutes. The time will depend on the thickness of the salmon.

Remove from the plank and serve with lemon wedges.

CRÈME FRAÎCHE

Mix all ingredients for the crème fraîche dressing and serve with a braaied avo.

BRAAIED AVOCADO

Brush avocado halves with olive oil. Season with salt. Braai, cut-side down, until black lines appear (about 3 minutes).

★ MOROCCAN LAMB ★
WITH BRAAIED PITAS AND TZATZIKI

Mechoui paste originates in North Africa where whole roast lamb is braaied on a spit. The meat is marinated in this wonderful spice paste, braaied until it's tender enough to be pulled apart with your fingers.

INGREDIENTS

1 deboned leg lamb, butterflied

MECHOUI MARINADE
Make the mechoui marinade in advance if you like.

125ml mint leaves, finely chopped

125ml coriander leaves, finely chopped

200ml lemon juice

15ml ground cumin

15ml crushed garlic

15ml sweet paprika

5ml dried chilli flakes

15ml ground coriander

3mg cinnamon

125ml olive oil

salt to taste

Combine all the ingredients in a bowl. Put the leg of lamb in a shallow dish. Pour mechoui over and leave to marinate for 1 hour.

Remove lamb from the marinade and place on an oiled grid.

Braai for 45 minutes to 1 hour. Remove and let it rest for 10 minutes.

Braai pita rounds on the fire under a griddle.

Mix all ingredients together in a bowl.

Serve with couscous salad from page 134 and the tzatziki from page 52.

★ SPANISH ★
BEEF FILLET

This beef fillet is ready when you are... braai it in advance and let it rest before slicing it.

INGREDIENTS

1.5kg beef fillet, trimmed of any fat and sinew

8 cloves garlic

250ml sherry

125ml red wine

60ml balsamic vinegar

4 bay leaves

10ml dried thyme

5ml smoked Spanish paprika

30ml olive oil

Cut the garlic into thin slivers. Make incisions all over the beef and put slivered garlic into the incisions. Put the beef fillet in a bowl and pour sherry, wine and balsamic over it. Add bay leaves. Cover and marinate, refrigerated, for a few hours. Turn the beef every hour. Remove from the fridge 1 hour before braaing. Drain from sherry–wine marinade. Discard bay leaves.

Place beef fillet on an oiled grid. Braai for 20 to 25 minutes, turning once. Place beef fillet in foil and let it rest on the coldest side of the braai.

Boil the sherry, wine and balsamic vinegar marinade until syrupy. You can add 15ml brown sugar. Unwrap the beef fillet. Slice into thin slices and drizzle sherry marinade over or put it in a small bowl.

Eish!

INGREDIENTS

800g – 1kg whole sirloin

30ml olive oil

1 onion, chopped

1 x 5cm fresh ginger, grated

1 red chilli, seeded
and chopped

2 cloves garlic, crushed

60ml Mrs Ball's chutney

60ml tomato sauce

15ml wholegrain mustard

30ml balsamic vinegar

1 x 340ml can Coca-Cola

60ml brandy

Heat the oil in a saucepan and fry the onion, garlic, chilli and ginger until softened. Add the remaining ingredients and simmer for 15 to 20 minutes. Cool completely.

Pour half of the brandy and Coke over the sirloin. Reserve the rest of the sauce. Marinate the sirloin, covered, in the refrigerator overnight. Drain off the marinade. Bring the meat to room temperature.

Put the sirloin on an oiled grid and braai for 25 to 30 minutes.

Rest for 5 minutes before slicing.

Serve with the reserved sauce, heated.

★ NO-FUSS ★
TURKEY

This amazingly simple festive recipe comes from one of my favourite cookbooks, 'Bloke' by Jason Comins

INGREDIENTS

1 x 5–6kg turkey

STUFFING

½ loaf stale white bread

2 onions, finely chopped

200g butter

25g fresh sage, finely chopped

50g flat-leaf parsley, finely chopped

200ml cream

50ml medium sherry (or port)

500ml white wine

hickory or cedar chips for the fire

Chunk the bread and blitz it in a blender with the crust on to make fine crumbs. Over a low heat, gently fry the onion in all the butter, until they soften (you want no browning to occur). Remove from the heat and add the breadcrumbs, herbs, cream and sherry. Stir to combine well.

When the stuffing is completely cool, you can stuff the bird. Loosen the skin over the breasts and pack in a handful of stuffing. You want an even layer about 1cm thick to keep the white meat from drying out. Take the rest of the stuffing and pack it into the cavity of the turkey.

Pour the white wine into the drip pan in your kettle braai. I use dry wine, but you can use whatever you like. It's there to keep the bird moist and to form the base of a gravy with all the lovely juices that drip into the pan. Scatter the woodchips on the coals on both sides, and place the turkey on the centre of the grid. Close the lid and leave for roughly 2 hours. Some frozen turkeys have thermometers that pop up when they are cooked. These make life very easy, but if you are cooking a fresh bird, the old trick of cutting between the leg and breast with a sharp knife works too. You want to see clear juices flowing there to know that the turkey is done.

SIDES
★ FROM THE ★
FIRE

PARCEL POTATOES
★ WITH AN ASIAN TWIST ★

Add these potato parcels to your braai while braaing meat or fish, using the indirect method.

INGREDIENTS

6 potatoes cut into 1cm cubes

80g butter

2 cloves garlic, crushed

50ml soy sauce

1 bunch spring onion, finely sliced

18 young French beans or mangetout

10ml sesame seeds

salt

Cut 6 sheets of heavy-duty foil, each approximately 30cm long. Place the foil shiny-side down. Spread some butter where the potatoes will be placed. Arrange the potatoes on the 6 parcels and sprinkle the remaining ingredients. Seal the parcels well.

Braai over indirect heat for 30 minutes. Remove from the braai. Let them rest for a few minutes before you open the parcels.

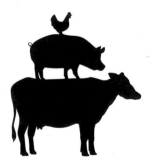

BBQ PANZANELLA SALAD

Italian bread salad known as Panzanella. A day-old ciabatta or focaccia bread is perfect for this recipe.

INGREDIENTS

3 red or yellow peppers

oil for brushing

2 loaves of stale ciabatta or focaccia, thickly sliced

1kg tomatoes

1 red onion, sliced

150g pitted black olives

60g capers, drained and rinsed

chopped Italian parsley and fresh basil leaves for garnish

PANZANELLA DRESSING

2 cloves garlic, crushed

15ml red wine vinegar

salt and freshly ground black pepper

tomato juice from the tomatoes

Mix together and reserve until needed.

Brush the peppers with oil and braai on direct, medium heat for 12 to 15 minutes, turning 2 to 3 times until blackened. Remove from the braai. Put in a plastic bag for 15 minutes to steam the skins. Peel the skins and slice the peppers into strips.

Braai the bread over direct, medium heat for 2 to 3 minutes, turning once until toasted and marked with the braai grid.

Halve the tomatoes and scoop out the seeds into a sieve set over a bowl to catch the juices. Put aside. Chop the tomatoes into pieces. Add tomatoes, peppers, capers, olives and red onion in a bowl.

Break the braaied bread into pieces and put in a clean bowl. Stir the garlic, olive oil, tomato juice and seasoning together and pour over the bread. Make sure the bread absorbs all juices.

Make layers of the soaked bread, peppers and tomato mix, and garnish with the fresh herbs.

★ ROOSTERKOEK ★

This is delicious with farm butter, so get to a good farmers' market soon.

INGREDIENTS

500ml cake flour
10ml baking powder
pinch of salt
pinch of sugar
250ml fresh cream
125ml water

Makes 12 to 15 roosterkoeke.

Sift the dry ingredients into a mixing bowl. Add the cream and water.

Knead and divide into little squares. Braai both sides on direct heat until squares are braaied through. As soon as they are done, remove from the braai and rub them with butter, as you do not want them to be too crispy. Eat with homemade apricot jam, grated cheddar cheese and farm butter.

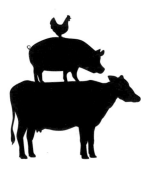

★ CHEESE AND ONION ★
CIDER BREAD

Mix and bake this easy bread recipe while the fire is getting ready.

INGREDIENTS

750ml self-raising flour

1 cider beer

100g cheddar cheese, grated

50g onion rings, fried in a olive oil, flavoured with thyme leaves, salt and pepper.

Preheat oven to 180°C. Mix all the ingredients in a bowl, but save a little cheese for the top.

Pour into a greased bread tin. Add onion rings and cheese to top. Bake for 50 to 60 minutes.

Insert pin after 45 minutes of baking. Cool and turn out onto a wire rack.

BRAAIED
★ GARLIC ★
MUSHROOMS

Mushrooms are perfect for the braai.
Use direct heat.

INGREDIENTS

8 brown mushrooms

Pesto oil

5ml garlic, crushed

200ml olive oil

15ml basil pesto

salt and freshly
ground black pepper

Brush the brown mushrooms with the basil oil.

Braai for 3 to 4 minutes each side, depending on the mushroom size.

Serve warm with fresh basil leaves, sliced baby tomatoes and feta cheese.

MEALIES ★
IN LIME, CHILLI AND CORIANDER BUTTER

I know, a simple grilled mealie with butter is completely delicious, but treat yourself to something new. You'll be hooked.

INGREDIENTS

4 corn on the cob

olive oil for brushing

LIME, CHILLI AND CORIANDER BUTTER

150g butter

salt and freshly ground black pepper

2 cloves garlic, chopped

1 red chilli, seeded and chopped

1 grated rind and juice of one lime

150ml chopped fresh coriander

Rub the sweetcorn with some oil and cook over direct heat, turning frequently for 10 to 12 minutes until cooked.

Combine all the ingredients for the butter in a bowl and mix well. Remove the sweetcorn from the braai and serve with the coriander butter.

BRAAI NOTE: Soak corn in cold water for 30 minutes prior to braaing. If not, you'll end up with some toast!

BRAAIED PEPPER, FETA AND ★ ORANGE SALAD ★

This salad is for the lazy summer days. Don't stop at braaied oranges... what about some peaches or nectarines?

INGREDIENTS

6 large red or yellow peppers

6 firm but ripe oranges

200ml feta

rocket, fresh basil and watercress

BALSAMIC HONEY DRESSING

125ml olive oil

45ml balsamic vinegar

45ml honey

Shake all the ingredients together.

Cook the peppers on the braai for about 20 minutes. Turn regularly until the skins are completely blackened and blistered. Place them in a plastic bag, seal and leave until cool enough to handle. Remove the blackened skin and seeds. Cut the peppers into long, thin strips. Halve the oranges and braai on the grid until caramelised. Mix rocket, basil and watercress in a bowl. Add the feta cheese and peppers. Pour the dressing over and garnish with the oranges.

BRAAI NOTE: Never wash the roasted peppers, as they will lose all their flavour. Don't stop at grilled oranges. Braai nectarines when in season with the salad (instead of the oranges).

★ ROASTED ★ VEGETABLES

Thread smaller types of vegetables on skewers. Otherwise be big and bold with the vegetables you roast on the fire.

INGREDIENTS

1 red pepper, halved, seeded and quartered

1 yellow pepper, halved, seeded and quartered

1 aubergine, cut lengthwise in 1cm slices

1 red onion, sliced in thick slices

4 baby marrow, cut in 1cm chunks

4 medium tomatoes, halved or vine-ripened tomatoes

BALSAMIC-PESTO DRESSING

125ml olive oil

60ml balsamic vinegar

1 clove garlic, crushed

10ml basil pesto

Braai the vegetables on direct, medium heat. It should not take longer than 15 minutes. Remember to cut the vegetables in chunks as you don't want them to fall through the braai grid. These beautiful veggies call for some basil pesto or fresh basil. Add some lettuce leaves and fresh herbs for a salad.

Make salad dressing in a screw-top jar and shake. Braai vegetables on a heated, oiled grid until slightly charred but still firm. Don't forget your tongs! Combine vegetables in a large glass bowl. Drizzle with balsamic–pesto dressing.

BRAAIED
PEAR, BILTONG AND FETA SALAD

I love biltong... even for breakfast.

INGREDIENTS

4 pears, quartered

250g feta cheese, crumbed

100g wet biltong

1 packet wild rocket

1 spring onion, chopped

honey to drizzle braaied pears

salt and freshly ground
black pepper

olive oil to brush pears

balsamic vinegar to
drizzle over salad

Quarter pears. Brush with olive oil and braai on a medium heat until caramelised. Take off the braai and drizzle with honey. Mix the feta cheese, rocket and spring onions together in a bowl. Drizzle with more olive oil and season. Add pears and some balsamic vinegar.

BRAAI NOTE: Serve a beautiful wedge of blue cheese instead of feta.

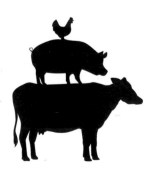

FIRE-ROASTED
★ ITALIAN ★
TOMATOES

These tomatoes can be served with any braaied meat or fish. The more you braai the outside of the tomatoes, the more smoky the flavour will be.

INGREDIENTS

4 ripe tomatoes, halved

15ml olive oil

salt and freshly ground
black pepper

pinch of brown sugar

fresh basil leaves, torn

Mix olive oil, salt and pepper and brown sugar in a bowl. Halve and coat the tomatoes. Braai them on medium to hot coals, flesh side down first, until lightly charred but still firm. Turn and repeat. Tear the fresh basil leaves over tomatoes to serve.

★ POTATO WEDGES ★

*Who doesn't love a potato on the braai?
No need to wrap them in foil, chuck
them on the fire and hope.
These are irresistible.*

INGREDIENTS

1kg potatoes, par-boiled
for 20 minutes

60ml olive oil

pinch of paprika and
dried thyme

salt and freshly ground
black pepper

Cut the potatoes into large chucks – we don't want them to fall through the grid.

Marinate in olive oil, paprika and thyme. Season. Use your tongs and braai for 10 to 15 minutes over direct, medium heat, turning once. Potatoes should be golden brown, crisp and braaied through.

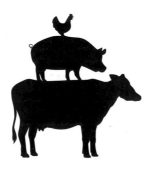

CHEESY GARLIC BREAD

An ordinary French loaf or baguette gets a makeover to become extraordinary.

INGREDIENTS

1 French loaf or baguette

150g butter, softened

4–6 cloves garlic, minced

30ml chopped flat-leaf parsley or basil leaves

75g basil pesto

75g tomato pesto

mozzarella cheese, sliced

Mix ingredients together for the garlic butter. Set aside.

Slice the bread at 2cm intervals, but do not cut all the way through.

Open each alternate slice and spread with the garlic and herb butter. Spread the pesto in the remaining slices. Place mozzarella slices in between each.

Wrap the bread in foil and heat over the braai for 15 to 20 minutes.

BRAAI NOTE: Brush some oil underneath the bread. This will prevent the bread from sticking.

SIDES
★ FROM THE ★
KITCHEN

★ POTATO BAKE ★

Potato bakes are sometimes my favourite thing at a braai. This one, dressed up with parmesan and cream, is just a killer.

INGREDIENTS

60g butter

3 large onions, finely chopped

6 large potatoes, peeled and thinly sliced

5ml paprika

salt and freshly ground black pepper

250ml fresh cream

60ml parmesan, grated

45ml breadcrumbs

30ml finely chopped basil or flat-leaf parsley

Preheat the oven to 180°C.

Heat the butter and sauté the onion until translucent. Set aside.

Wipe the potatoes with paper towel to remove their moisture.

When dried, place in a greased ovenware dish with the sautéed onions.

Season to taste.

Pour half the cream over and bake in the oven for 15 minutes.

Remove from the oven and add the rest of the cream.

Mix the parmesan, breadcrumbs and herbs together.

Sprinkle over the potatoes and bake for a further 25 to 30 minutes.

The cream should be absorbed, the potatoes soft and golden brown.

★ HERB AND FETA ★
CORN BREAD

From the kitchen to the braai in under one hour.

INGREDIENTS

150g yellow polenta

100g plain flour

5ml salt

a good grinding of freshly ground black pepper

30ml baking powder

15ml castor sugar

15ml chopped flat-leaf parsley or basil or a combination of the 2

1 red chilli, seeded and finely chopped

50g freshly grated parmesan

250ml buttermilk

2 large eggs, beaten

30ml olive oil

150g feta cheese, crumbled

olives, pipped and halved

Preheat the oven to 180°C. Grease a loaf tin (22x7cm).

In a bowl, add polenta, flour, salt, baking powder and castor sugar. Grind some pepper into the dry mix. Add the herbs, chilli and parmesan. Mix together. Beat together the buttermilk, eggs and olive oil. Mix the liquid into the dry ingredients quickly and briefly. Don't over-mix, but make sure that all ingredients are blended together. Stir in the feta cheese.

Pour dough into the prepared tin, sprinkle with olives and bake for 40 minutes until golden and a skewer is clean when pierced. Cool in the tin for 10 minutes, then turn out and leave to cool on a wire rack.

KITCHEN TIP: The parmesan cheese in the dough may burn the crust of the bread, so turn the oven down a bit after 30 minutes of baking.

★ BEER BREAD ★

Everyone is talking about craft beer and small brewers right now. Making bread with a great craft beer will be a show-stopper.

INGREDIENTS

750ml all-purpose flour

15ml sugar

15ml baking powder

5ml salt

5ml dried thyme

45ml honey

1 bottle beer

90g unsalted butter, melted

Preheat oven to 180°C. Grease a 23x13x7cm loaf tin. In a medium bowl, whisk together the flour, sugar, baking powder, salt, thyme and honey. Add the beer and stir with a wooden spoon until combined. Spread the batter evenly in the prepared tin loaf and drizzle the melted butter over the batter. Bake for 50 to 60 minutes, then cool on a wire rack.

ROAST BUTTERNUT
★ AND CASHEW SALAD ★

Braaing butternut on your braai is no different from baking it in your oven. All you need is some foil to wrap the two halves in and a few magical ingredients.

INGREDIENTS

1 butternut, half lengthwise

60ml olive oil

125ml honey

salt and pepper

a bunch of rocket leaves

WHOLEGRAIN MUSTARD DRESSING

60ml wholegrain mustard

60ml pouring cream

250ml cup egg mayonnaise,

15ml lemon juice

5ml salt

Whisk all ingredients together.

Lightly toast cashews in a pan over medium heat.

Lay the butternut on its side on a chopping board and cut in half lengthwise. Scoop out any seeds. Drizzle olive oil over the two halves and rub with your fingers to ensure the butternut is coated. Season with salt and pepper. Drizzle the honey over the two halves. Wrap each butternut half in foil. Place face-down on the braai. Braai for 20 to 25 minutes on medium heat, turning once. Rest the butternut. Remove the butternut from the foil onto a platter. Pour any juices over from the foil. Scatter the cashew nuts over the butternut with some rocket. Serve the wholegrain mustard dressing on the side.

★ COS SALAD ★
WITH ANCHOVY DRESSING

This looks like a strange combination, but I borrowed it from a classic Caesar salad and it is sensational.

INGREDIENTS

1 head cos lettuce, washed and dried

1 clove garlic, crushed

2 anchovy fillets, rinsed and patted dry

30ml lemon juice

60ml cup olive oil

salt and freshly ground black pepper

250g parmesan cheese, shaved

Separate cos lettuce leaves. Cut crosswise but not through. Shave the parmesan cheese with a vegetable peeler. In a blender, purée garlic, anchovies and lemon juice. While the motor is running, add olive oil in a stream until emulsified. Season and toss lettuce with the dressing in a bowl. Add half the parmesan and season again. Add the rest of the parmesan shavings on top.

STRAWBERRY, FETA AND ★ POMEGRANATE SALAD ★

In the heart of summer I serve this beautiful strawberry and feta salad with lamb.

INGREDIENTS

200g strawberries, sliced in ¼

250g feta cheese, cubed

60g pomegranate pearls

fresh mint leaves

olive oil

Place ingredients in a bowl, drizzle with olive oil and season. Serve with ready-bought balsamic glaze.

PASTA AND PEA SALAD

The idea for this salad stems from the Genoa pasta dish using potatoes, steamed green beans and basil pesto. I call it the deli salad, as you can add any ingredients you like.

INGREDIENTS

350g cooked penne

60ml pesto

100g French beans

salt and freshly ground black pepper

Bring a pot of water to the boil, add salt and oil. Cook pasta until al dente (6 to 7 minutes). Drain the pasta and add to the pesto. Plunge green beans into hot, salted boiling water for 4 to 5 minutes. Strain and rinse until cold water. Add to the penne pesto.

Season with salt and freshly ground black pepper. Now add your deli desires – chopped sundried tomatoes, pitted black olives, roasted red peppers, shavings of parmesan, mozzarella broken into pieces, fresh basil, rocket leaves – and drizzle with olive oil.

CHUNKY POTATO SALAD

Every household has their favourite potato salad — this is mine! Braai the bacon strips over hot coals if you feel adventurous.

INGREDIENTS

5 medium potatoes

1 red onion, coarsely chopped

4 rashers bacon, chopped

250ml of mayonnaise

15ml basil pesto

pitted black olives to taste

sundried tomatoes in olive oil to taste

4 hard-boiled eggs, halved

Boil the eggs for 8 minutes in boiling water.

Slice potatoes coarsely and cook in salted water till soft. Fry the onion with the bacon in a pan until crispy. Mix the mayonnaise with the pesto. When the potatoes are cooked, drizzle with olive oil and season while they are still piping hot. Add the bacon and onion mixture, chopped olives and sundried tomatoes to the potatoes along with the pesto mayonnaise and mix to coat evenly. You want the hot potatoes to drink in the dressing. Top with the egg and more basil pesto mayonnaise.

MUSTARD GREEN BEAN SALAD

Lightly cooked French beans make a beautiful salad; only be careful not to add lemon juice until just before serving as it will lose its vibrant colour. French beans don't need tailing, only topping. The tails are edible.

INGREDIENTS

200g green beans, trimmed
250g cherry tomatoes, halved
1 small red onion, thinly sliced

WHOLEGRAIN MUSTARD–ALMOND DRESSING

70g toasted almonds
30ml olive oil
30ml cider vinegar
5ml wholegrain mustard

Boil the beans until tender. Drain and rinse under cold water, drain again.

Mix olive oil, vinegar and wholegrain mustard in a small bowl. Toast almonds lightly in a small pan until lightly toasted.

Combine beans, tomato, onion rings and dressing in a bowl, toss gently. Scatter almonds over salad.

COUSCOUS ★ SALAD ★

Let's forget rice salads for a change and think light, nutty and full of flavour. Couscous requires almost no cooking, so it's perfect for a hot day! Strain tinned chickpeas well and add a lot of salt to the chickpeas for flavour.

INGREDIENTS

125ml olive oil
375ml couscous
60g almonds
1 tin chickpeas, drained
30g raisins, chopped
1 red onion, thinly sliced
125ml pomegranate pearls
250ml chopped coriander
60ml mint leaves
90ml lemon juice
1 clove garlic, crushed

Put 375ml water in a large saucepan and bring to the boil. Add 60ml olive oil and 5ml salt. Remove from the heat. Add the couscous. Cover with a lid for a few minutes. Fluff up the couscous with a fork. Stir in the almonds, chickpeas, raisins, red onion, pomegranate pearls and fresh herbs. Combine remaining olive oil with the lemon juice and garlic, and pour over salad. Season with salt and freshly ground black pepper.

KITCHEN NOTE: Add halved baby tomatoes, sliced cucumber and olives to this salad. I love preserved lemons with my couscous salad but they're not easily available. Use pomegranate pearls instead.

PAWPAW, BRAAIED LIME AND CHILLI SALAD

While working on the book, food stylist Camilla Comins made this beautiful, interesting salad. Thank you, Camilla.

INGREDIENTS

2 medium pawpaw, peeled and sliced

2 mozzarella balls, sliced

1 red chilli, sliced

3 limes, halved

125ml sweet chilli sauce

125ml olive oil

bunch of fresh coriander, chopped

Mix ingredients for the chilli dressing and set aside. Braai lime halves until charred.

Arrange pawpaw, mozzarella and sliced red chilli on a platter. Spoon the sweet chilli dressing over. Serve with the braaied limes.

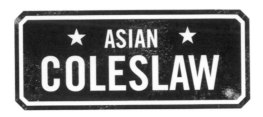

★ ASIAN ★
COLESLAW

This is not the coleslaw laden with mayonnaise that's been doing the rounds for over 200 years. Instead it's a fresh, Japanese-inspired salad laced with Eastern ingredients. I'll forgive you if you run to your local supermarket to purchase a packet of cabbage and carrot... Grate some beetroot at least...

INGREDIENTS

¼ green cabbage, finely sliced

¼ red cabbage, finely sliced

4 spring onions, finely sliced

1 large carrot, julienned

½ cucumber, julienned

1 beetroot, julienned or grated

30ml soy sauce

125ml rice vinegar

3 garlic cloves, crushed

1 x 5cm fresh ginger, finely grated

60ml cup brown sugar

15ml sesame oil

15ml vegetable oil

15ml peanut oil

60ml toasted sesame seeds

Put the cabbage, spring onion, carrot, cucumber and beetroot in a bowl.

Put the rest of the ingredients (except the sesame seeds) in a small bowl and whisk until the sugar has dissolved. Pour the dressing over the coleslaw and toss to coat all the vegetables. Refrigerate for a minimum of 1 hour. Just before serving, toast the sesame seeds over a low heat in a pan. Sprinkle over the salad and serve.

★ TOMATO RELISH ★

I call this my Bo-Kaap relish and it has a flavour that is pure Cape Town for me.

INGREDIENTS

15ml sunflower oil

15ml yellow mustard seeds

6 dried curry leaves

1 onion, sliced

2 garlic cloves, chopped

15ml each ground coriander, turmeric

250ml brown sugar

250ml white vinegar

2 x 400g whole tomatoes, drained

salt and freshly ground black pepper

Heat the oil in a saucepan over medium heat. Add the mustard seeds and curry leaves. Heat the mustard seeds until they pop. Add the onion and garlic and quickly fry. Don't burn! Add the remaining ingredients and reduce until it forms a thick, sweet-and-sour and jammy relish. Season.

BEETROOT ★RELISH★

This beetroot relish is a staple in my kitchen. It can be stored in the fridge for up to 2 months.

INGREDIENTS

750g beetroot, peeled and coarsely grated

300g castor sugar

1 onion, chopped finely

375ml balsamic vinegar

250ml water

15ml yellow mustard seeds

1 x 7cm piece orange rind

250ml freshly squeezed orange juice

salt

Place all ingredients in a pot. Cook over medium heat, cover and bring to the boil. Cook for 30 minutes until liquid has reduced and thickened slightly. Spoon into sterilised jars and seal.

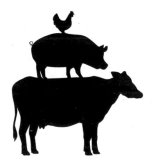

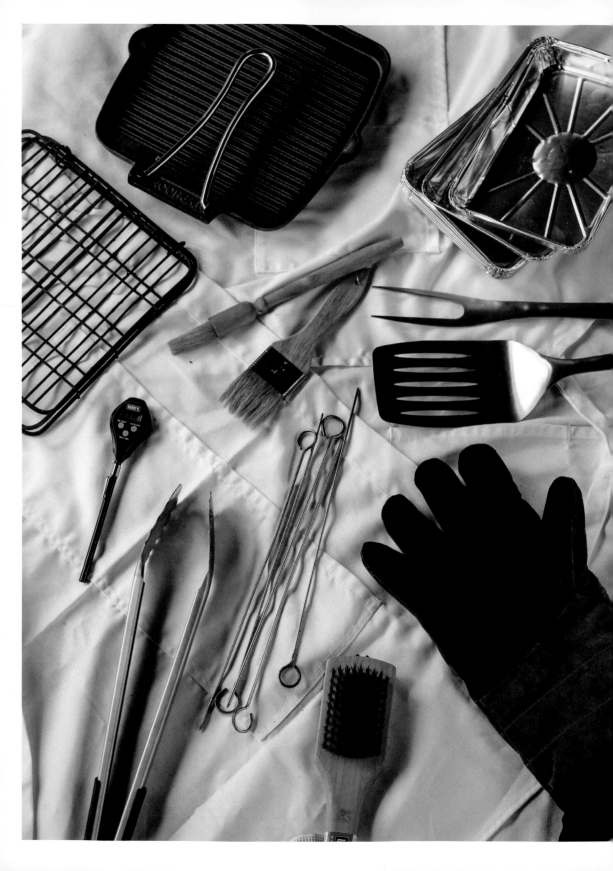

Foil drip tray – will keep the base of the kettle braai clean and gather juices, fats and braai bastes that fall from the food during braaing.

Braai fork – this should be long and sturdy to handle meats such as leg of lamb. However, avoid stabbing the meat with it.

Stainless steel spatula – This should be broad enough and strong enough to flip anything from a burger to a whole fish. Look out for the sharp-edged spatulas – they are the best.

Oversized braai glove – Braais get hot, very hot! Braaing will be smooth with one or two of these gloves. Gloves should be long-sleeved and flame-resistant.

Grill brush – Before and after you use your braai, give it a good scrape with a metal brush. Forget about the dishwasher this time!

Metal skewers – Long and strong is what you want. They will keep sosaties and vegetables in place.

Tongs – Mine are sturdy, stainless steel and indispensable. Yours should be too. Make sure the handle is long enough to reach all the way to the back of the braai.

Instant-read thermometer – Take the temperature. To prevent disaster with that expensive meat, nothing beats this gadget. Read the instructions when you purchase it. Remember to insert it into the thickest part of the meat without letting it touch bone.

Hinged grid – The handy wire braai contraption. It's common sense to braai a whole fish with this.

Flat plate or griddle plate – Can be used on the braai or in oven. Use the flat plate for calamari, haloumi or chorizo for instance.

Basting brush – The ultimate flavour-enhancing tool. Baste ribs or salmon with your favourite sauce or marinade.

★ JEAN'S ★
KITCHEN
BASICS

Great meat equals great flavour!
However, it'll be lost without these ingredients!

Olive oil and extra virgin olive oil for salads

Tomato sauce and Mrs Ball's Chutney for enhancing marinades and sauces

Sweet chilli sauce as a basting

Fresh ginger, garlic and chilli for everything

Wholegrain mustard rubbed on a piece of meat or mixed with mayonnaise

Lemon juice is always fresh

Salt is always sea salt flakes or kosher salt

Pepper is always freshly ground or crushed in a pestle

Fresh herbs – the harder herbs such as rosemary and sage for marinades and the softer herbs such as fresh basil leaves, dancing seductively

Fresh bay leaves for marinades and as a flavourant for sosaties

Basil pesto is always freshly made as it adds punchy flavours to your dish

Organic dried herbs and spices are more pungent, potent and flavoursome

I always have feta cheese and Danish feta for salads

Invest in a good chef's knife – it will last for a long time

A pestle and mortar to crush peppercorns, spices and blend pastes

Plenty of kitchen lappies – I go through dozens

INGREDIENTS

10ml paprika

10ml castor sugar

10ml brown sugar

10ml dried chilli flakes

10ml salt

5ml dried thyme

5ml cumin

5ml black pepper

Get ready for the delightful aromas when braaing meat or chicken with this rub.

Mix all the ingredients together and store till needed.

INGREDIENTS

1 can Coca-Cola

250ml tomato sauce

15ml Worcestershire sauce

15ml dry mustard

60ml white wine vinegar

30ml HP sauce

15ml Mrs Ball's chutney

5ml Tabasco (optional)

I frowned upon using Coca-Cola in sauces until I made this one. It may change your life too...

Bring all the ingredients to the boil, reduce and simmer for 18 to 20 minutes. Stir occasionally. Sauce should have a thick red colour.

CLEANING THE BRAAI AND TOOLS

CARING FOR THE CAST IRON POT/PAN

It is important to clean your braai to make it last. After all, you clean your kitchen after you've cooked dinner, don't you? Greasy, dirty braais are not only a health hazard, but also a fire hazard. Look after your braai and it will return the favour for many summers... or winters, or every day.

KETTLE BRAAIS

Kettle braais need to cool down COMPLETELY before cleaning.

Sweep all ash into the bottom tray and discard. The cold ash is fantastic for your garden!

Remove both wire racks and rub gently with a wire brush.

Wipe the vents of kettle braais frequently to make sure that they are clean and that air can flow freely through wide open vents. Scrape off any grime with a brush or hot water (never soapy water). Dry thoroughly with newspaper or a damp cloth.

Wash inside and outside of the kettle. Dry with newspaper.

Put it back together until the next braai.

HINGED BRAAI GRIDS

Heat the grid over the coals. Take away from the heat. Pick it up and knock on the side of the braai to remove any rough debris.

First published by Jacana Media (Pty) Ltd in 2013

10 Orange Street
Sunnyside
Auckland Park 2092
South Africa
+2711 628 3200
www.jacana.co.za

© Jean Nel, 2013

All rights reserved.

ISBN 978-1-4314-0908-2

Photographs by Russel Wasserfall
Braai the Beloved Country shot on location at
Marianne Wine Estate near Stellenbosch
Design by Shawn Paikin
Set in Stempel Garamond 10.5/16pt
Printed and bound by Craft Print International Ltd
Job no. 002076

See a complete list of Jacana titles at www.jacana.co.za